This book is to be returned
or before the date stamped b

D1765874

UNIVERSITY OF PLYMOUTH

EXMOUTH LIBRARY

Tel: (01395) 255331

This book is subject to recall if required by another reader
Books may be renewed by phone
CHARGES WILL BE MADE FOR OVERDUE BOOKS

Intermediate Appellate Courts: Improving Case Processing

Final Report

Submitted to the State Justice Institute

by

National Center for State Courts

JOY A. CHAPPER
Co-Project Director

ROGER A. HANSON
Co-Project Director

April 1990

This report was developed under grant SJI-88-08G-B-071 from the State Justice
Institute. Points of view expressed herein are those of the authors and do not
necessarily represent the official position or policies of the State Justice Institute.

KF
8736
I59
1990
Cp.2

Acknowledgments

A number of individuals have helped to produce this comparative examination of state intermediate appellate courts. Judges, staff, and attorneys in each of the four research sites gave generously of their time in discussing appellate court issues, resolving data collection problems, and in reviewing the project's results. Special thanks are given to Chief Judge Sarah D. Grant and Glen D. Clark, clerk, Arizona Court of Appeals, Division One; Chief Judge Monterey Campbell III and William A. Haddad, clerk, Florida Second District Court of Appeal; Chief Judge Richard P. Gilbert and Leslie D. Gradet, clerk, Maryland Court of Special Appeals; and Presiding Judge for Administration Herman D. Michels and John Musewicz, appellate division administrator, Appellate Division of the New Jersey Superior Court, for their cooperation, which facilitated all phases of the research.

An advisory committee composed of Judge Harriet Lansing, Minnesota Court of Appeals; Judge Leonard P. Plank, Colorado Court of Appeals; Richard B. Hoffman, clerk, District of Columbia Court of Appeals; and Professor David Neubauer, University of New Orleans, appreciably improved the quality of the research. Their helpful advice contributed to the organization, substance, and style of this report.

Colleagues at the National Center for State Courts and elsewhere provided constructive criticisms of the project's methodology and findings. Their comments helped strengthen the final report in a variety of ways. Appreciation is extended to Victor Flango, Geoff Gallas, John Goerdt, William Hewitt, Susan Keilitz, Kenneth Pankey, and David Rottman for their suggestions; and to Stevalynn Adams, Charles Campbell, Bill Fishback, Mary McCall, and Hisako Sayers of the Center's publication service.

Finally, the support of the State Justice Institute in sponsoring the research is much appreciated. In particular, the careful monitoring by Ms. Daina Farthing-Capowich brought the project to a pleasant conclusion.

Project Staff

Joy Chapper	Roger Hanson	Craig Boersema
Brian Lynch	Deborah Gause	Richard Semiatin

iii

Executive Summary

The state intermediate appellate court (IAC) is a new, growing, and evolving institution. As recently as 1957, IACs existed in only 13 states. However, by the end of the 1980s, 37 states had permanent IACs, one state had a temporary IAC, and additional jurisdictions were considering creating them.

IACs are primarily courts of mandatory jurisdiction, hearing appeals of right filed from decisions of the trial court. Because few of their decisions are reviewed by the court of last resort, IACs are, in fact if not in law, the final arbiter of most cases. Despite the key role IACs play in maintaining the accountability of the trial court process, very little is known about them. The lack of systematic knowledge about these courts has important consequences. Without detailed information, individual courts cannot identify with precision where problems exist or what opportunities for self-improvement are appropriate.

This report provides information from the first comparative study devoted exclusively to IACs in an effort to address basic unanswered questions concerning their operations:

- *Caseload*: What do appeals look like? Do differences in jurisdiction affect caseload composition? To what extent do appeals wash out before being decided by the court? Is the attrition greater for civil than criminal appeals?
- *Procedure*: What steps in the traditional appellate process are modified? How are traditional procedures altered and for what kinds of cases? How do courts ensure that quality is preserved when modifications are introduced?
- *Case Processing*: Do particular stages of the appellate process, such as record preparation and briefing, take longer than other stages? Do the same patterns hold true for both civil and criminal appeals? Are particular case characteristics associated with the time that it takes to resolve

cases? Do procedures, such as oral argument and the publication of opinions, affect case processing time?

Four courts serve as research sites, providing data on appeals filed in 1986 and 1987. They are the Arizona Court of Appeals, Division One in Phoenix; the Florida Second District Court of Appeal in Lakeland; the Maryland Court of Special Appeals; and the New Jersey Superior Court, Appellate Division.

Ten essential findings from the four-court inquiry are highlighted below:

(1) Although the jurisdiction of IACs is primarily mandatory, study of the four courts indicates that there are considerable differences in the right of appeal, particularly from nontrial criminal matters, which result in some courts avoiding categories of appeals that constitute an appreciable part of the caseload of other courts.

(2) Despite differences in jurisdiction, the four courts are similar in caseload composition in terms of the areas of underlying civil law and the most serious criminal offense at conviction. The most striking aspect of the caseload composition is that the percentage of criminal appeals where the most serious offense is drug sale or possession is striking: 23 percent of the caseload in Florida and New Jersey and 16 percent in Arizona and Maryland.

(3) The volume of appeals filed or docketed overstates a court's actual workload as a sizable volume of appeals are dismissed or abandoned before they reach the court for consideration. A funnel-like case attrition occurs even where a court does not encourage the early resolution of appeals.

(4) The alteration of one or more of the basic steps in the appellate process is widespread, with some modifications (e.g., the submission on the briefs without oral argument and unpublished decisions) being seen in every court.

(5) The time consumed by the appeals process is not uniform across courts or within courts for criminal and civil cases. Nonetheless, criminal appeals generally take longer to reach perfection than civil appeals, and much of this difference is attributable to the time taken for the appellant to file an opening brief.

(6) In criminal appeals, the only factor consistently related to appeal time is the type of offense at conviction. Appeals from homicide convictions take the longest, followed by those from other crimes against the person, and then those involving all other offenses.

(7) In civil appeals, the underlying trial court proceeding is related to appeal time. Appeals from jury trials take the longest amount of time, followed by those from nonjury trials and all other proceedings. Areas of civil law (e.g., tort, contract, domestic relations) do not distinguish fast appeals from slow ones.

(8) The use of oral argument does not consistently affect appeal time for either civil or criminal cases. Instead, if courts are expeditious in handling cases at the stage between the close of briefing and argument or submission without argument, then they are expeditious for both argued and nonargued appeals.

(9) Publishing an opinion adds to decision time for both civil and criminal appeals.

(10) The principles of case management distilled from the trial court experience have clear parallels in appellate court case processing. However, these principles will not be applied fully until information systems are organized to provide information upon which appropriate management decisions can be based.

These findings have a number of implications for improving case processing by IACs. First, they reveal the importance of understanding context when making cross-court comparisons. Because differences in subject matter jurisdiction contribute to variations in caseload composition, affecting the extent to which appeals ultimately reach the court for decision, courts need to know how their context compares to that of others in determining whether a procedure used elsewhere will be appropriate or will require adjustment.

Second, the experiences of Arizona, Florida, Maryland, and New Jersey imply that traditional appellate procedures can be modified without affecting quality. However, special procedures need to be viewed in context to see what makes the modification feasible and how quality is maintained.

Third, although a potential problem confronting all courts is delay in the briefing of criminal appeals and, more specifically, the filing of the appellant's brief by an appellate defender, some jurisdictions have had success in treating resource shortages as management issues and have responded with procedures that enable them to maximize available resources. This includes counsel's active exploration with appellant of alternatives to an appeal and the court's adoption of procedures that eliminate or abbreviate brief writing, circumvent bottlenecks in the defender's office, and accelerate the court's consideration of certain categories of appeals.

Finally, one way for IACs to maintain greater accountability, monitor their performance more closely, and take necessary corrective measures is by obtaining systematic information on their operations and outcomes. The unavailability of information on caseload composition, attrition rates, and case processing time inhibits clear problem identification and choice of promising solutions.

Similarly, the transfer of innovative ideas and approaches across courts would be encouraged by comparative information on court procedures and the circumstances in which they are used. For example, although courts vary widely in the frequency of *Anders* briefs (they are not recognized in Maryland and are filed in over half of all criminal appeals in Arizona), there is no systematic information on the procedures courts follow in these kinds of cases. Such comparative information is also lacking on "fast tracks," appellate settlement conferences, the use of staff attorneys, and other specialized procedures. Having systematic descriptive information would make innovative procedures more comprehensible and encourage their consideration. Thus, individual IACs should be assisted in enhancing their own management information systems and supported by research aimed at problems that are national in scope.

Contents

Introduction

A major development in the organization of American state court systems over the past three decades has been the establishment and growth of intermediate appellate courts (IACs). Only 13 states had intermediate appellate courts in 1957, but by the end of the 1980s 37 states had permanent IACs, North Dakota had a temporary IAC, and additional jurisdictions were considering their establishment.

Once established, IACs expand in size, as seen by the fact that 11 states now have over 20 judges serving in courts at this level. The larger courts also show a tendency to be divided into regional units. At the end of 1988, for example, the largest IAC was the California Court of Appeal, which had 88 judges in 6 districts. The 80-judge Texas Court of Appeals is divided into 14 districts, the Ohio Court of Appeals has 59 judges in 12 locations, and the Louisiana Court of Appeals has 52 judges in 5 circuits.

When an IAC is created, appeals from decisions of the trial court go to the IAC for review instead of directly to the court of last resort (COLR).[1] The IAC thus takes on a primarily mandatory jurisdiction, enabling the COLR, with an increased discretionary jurisdiction, to focus on the cases and issues of overarching importance. But because few of the IAC's decisions are reviewed by the COLR, they are, in fact if not in law, the final arbiter for most cases.[2] Hence, IACs are crucial to maintaining accountability over trial court actions and decisions.

Basic Problems Confronting Intermediate Appellate Courts

Limited attention has been given to IACs in large measure because they have only recently become part of the American court landscape. They were seen, and still may be seen by some, simply as solutions to the problems of COLRs, whose backlog and delay problems they were created to relieve (see

Kagan et al., 1978; Stookey, 1982). However, once IACs are viewed as institutions in their own right, a set of questions arises concerning their activities. What kinds of cases are they called on to resolve? Are all cases handled under the traditional appellate process? If not, how do courts preserve quality when they modify the traditional process to increase productivity? How do courts perform in terms of the basic performance standard of processing cases expeditiously?

The importance of these questions is accentuated by several factors indicating that IACs are in serious need of special attention. Those factors include the following:

- The volume of work IACs handle is substantial because of their primarily mandatory jurisdiction. Studies have concluded that during the 1970s and the early 1980s, the number of cases on appeal nationwide doubled every 8 to 10 years (Flango and Elsner, 1983; Marvell and Lindgren, 1985). Caseloads continued to rise through the 1980s, although the rate of increase was less than in the prior decade (National Center for State Courts, 1990).
- Solutions that in the 1970s seemed reasonable to demands for greater productivity are now under reconsideration. For example, the recommended use of central staff (see Carrington et al., 1976) has been questioned by states that originally pioneered this innovation (e.g., Michigan), even as other courts are increasing their use of staff assistance.
- Procedures adopted by some individual courts in the early 1980s to reduce court costs and delay have not taken hold elsewhere (Wasby, 1987). Reform may have become immobilized in part because of concerns that due process is impaired when cases are handled under procedures that modify the traditional appellate process (Davies, 1981, 1982). While this criticism has been shown to lack empirical support (Chapper and Hanson, 1988), it has led some judges to believe that procedures designed to increase court efficiency (including differentiated case management) may sacrifice quality (e.g., Thompson, 1987).
- The performance of IACs is in the spotlight because of recently adopted American Bar Association (ABA) time Standards for Appeals. The standards prescribe how long appeals should take from the filing of the notice of appeal to final disposition. Although there is some ambiguity concerning the exact nature of the ABA's time standards, in many IACs appeals are not resolved within the standards' 280-day limit.[3]

Although these problems are serious, they are tractable. Systematic research can inform judges and attorneys of their options to improve the handling of civil and criminal appeals.

Research Agenda

Intermediate appellate courts currently confront increasing caseloads and will continue to do so. Because no single paradigm to managing appeals has emerged, solutions are more the product of opinion and conjecture and lack systematic empirical support. Research can help to improve case processing by addressing issues that revolve around the special needs of IACs.

Caseload

There is a need for systematic information on the present caseload composition of IACs. Because these courts vary in their jurisdiction and their relationships with the other courts in their state (see National Center for State Courts, 1985), it is not self-evident that they are handling the same kinds of cases.

One of the most commonly mentioned characterizations of appeals is that much of the work of IACs is routine rather than complex in nature (Wold and Caldeira, 1980; Wold, 1978). As a result, IACs are viewed as serving an error-correcting function, with the COLRs performing more of a legal policy function (see also Baum, 1977). This general assertion that most cases are routine and few are complex lacks evidence based on the objective characteristics of the caseload. What percentage of civil appeals involve domestic relations matters compared to either tort actions or reviews of agency actions? What percentage of criminal appeals involve convictions of serious offenses as compared to relatively minor ones? How many appeals are from trials rather than other proceedings?

Procedure

There have been efforts to describe how some courts have designed specific procedures, such as no-argument calendars and fast tracks, to deal with a particular portion of their caseload (Chapper and Hanson, 1983, 1988; Olson and Chapper, 1983; Douglas, 1985). Because these studies do not describe the full range of procedures that the courts have in place, there is a need for a more complete picture of the extent to which courts modify the traditional appellate process. How are steps in the appellate process altered? To what extent have IACs moved toward differentiated procedures? What has been the effect of these changes on case processing?

Case Processing

The processing of cases on appeal needs to be better understood. The only comparative study of time on appeal[4] was conducted over a decade ago (see Martin and Prescott, 1981), and it is uncertain whether its conclusions still hold.[5] One such conclusion was that because the same casetype was not consistently the fastest (or the slowest) across the 10 appellate courts studied, case characteristics are unrelated to the length of case processing time. Because of the implications of this conclusion for the management of IACs, it is important to test this observation and determine whether it remains valid. Do appeals in tort cases or homicide cases take longer than appeals arising in different areas of law or involving convictions for other offenses? Does it make a difference in appeal time whether the case below was resolved by a trial rather than a nontrial proceeding?

These research issues indicate the importance of building strategies for improved case processing on an empirical foundation. Systematic information concerning caseload composition and court procedures can illustrate the search for solutions to problems.

Project Objectives

The lack of systematic knowledge about the work of IACs inhibits appellate reform activity. Without empirical groundwork, IACs cannot link one of many possible ideas for reform to their particular circumstances. To begin to address this need for systematic information, the National Center for State Courts designed the first comparative study devoted exclusively to state intermediate appellate courts. The four courts involved in this study are the Arizona Court of Appeals, Division One, in Phoenix; the Florida Second District Court of Appeal in Lakeland; the Maryland Court of Special Appeals; and the New Jersey Superior Court, Appellate Division. Hereinafter, these courts are called Arizona, Florida, Maryland, and New Jersey.

This research project has three objectives. First, it is to provide an empirical foundation to improve intermediate appellate courts by describing the kinds of cases that can be, and those that are in fact, brought on appeal in the courts under study. Second, the project highlights what courts can do to improve case processing by examining caseload pressures in the research sites. Third, it increases understanding of what accounts for expeditious case processing.

The project's research results have implications both for the four courts under study and for other IACs across the country. First, the study's analytical framework and results should give each IAC a structured way of viewing and understanding its own situation. What is the aggregate picture of trends over time in caseload composition? For example, are drug cases adding to volume and complexity of the caseload? Second, the study's comparative methodology gives courts an opportunity to see how they stand in relation to others. How similar to or different from other courts are they in subject matter jurisdiction? Do differences in subject matter jurisdiction affect caseload composition? What sorts of procedures have courts adopted in response to caseload pressures? What procedures look relevant and promising as tools for improved management? Finally, the results shed light on the role of the court's management structure and the use of staff in the introduction of new procedures. How can courts best implement and institutionalize settlement conferences, delay reduction programs, differentiated case management, or other ideas?

The four courts reflect broad diversity on a number of dimensions. The Maryland and New Jersey courts have statewide jurisdiction; the other two are regional appellate courts. In the Arizona court, the majority of the appeals come from a single metropolitan area (Phoenix); in the Florida court, a sizable number of appeals come from outside the cities of Tampa and St. Petersburg. The New Jersey court, with 28 judges, is the largest IAC in the country with one administrative office.

In each court, the project drew a random sample of 1,000 civil and criminal appeals filed in 1986 and 1987. Case records provided information on the case in the lower court, the number and length of briefs filed, counsel on appeal, issues raised on appeal, and outcome of the appeal. Information on procedural events, including elapsed time, also came from case records. The examination of administrative records provided information on structural factors including caseload, workload, and staffing ratios. Site visits provided information on the existence of alternative procedures and the dynamics of their use. Interviews with presiding judges, clerks of court, principal staff attorneys, and members of the bar provided information on management approaches and attitudes and views regarding a variety of alternative procedures.[6]

The findings of this research and a discussion of their implications are set out in the following chapters. The first chapter looks at the work of IACs, focusing on differences in their subject matter jurisdiction, caseload composition, and attrition rate. The second chapter lays out appellate court procedures, with special attention to modifications of the traditional appellate process, why they came into being, and the considerations of quality involved in their use. These two chapters provide the necessary background for the succeeding chapter, which looks at case processing time for decided appeals and the extent to which case characteristics and procedural factors explain differences in appeal time both within a court and across courts. The final chapter integrates key findings and discusses their implications for improving case processing in intermediate appellate courts.

Separate appendices present an in-depth examination of each of the four courts. These case studies provide more detailed information on the court context and procedures for the reader who has a special interest in one of the topics raised in the body of the report. The appendices may also be consulted for further explanation of court-specific procedures referred to in the narrative.